OPTIONS MADE EASY

HOW TO MAKE PROFITS TRADING IN PUTS AND CALLS

W.D. GANN

Cover Design: J.Neuman

CONTENTS

PREFACE

To make a success trading in stocks every man should learn everything he can about the stock market and the ways to operate in the market in order to make the greatest success. He should learn to take the smallest risk possible and then try to make the greatest profits possible. The more a man studies and learns the greater success he will have. We quote Proverbs 1: 5— "The wise man will Increase learning." Again, Proverbs 2: 11— "Discretion shall preserve these; understanding shall keep thee. "Proverbs 3: 9— "Give instructions to a wise man and he will become wiser. Teach a just man and he will increase in learning." The "Book of the Lambs" says that the fear of the market is the beginning of knowledge.

Many people do not realize that without

preparation and knowledge the stock market is dangerous and that it is easier to make losses than it is to make profits. However, the risks in stock speculation or investment are no greater than in any other line of business if you understand and apply the proper rules to speculative trading, and the profits compared to risks are greater than in any other business.

WHAT ARE PUTS AND CALLS ON STOCKS

PUTS and CALLS are insurance which provide protection for your profits and permit you to trade in stocks with limited risk. A CALL is a contract between you and the seller whereby he agrees to sell you a stock at a fixed price and deliver it in 30 days. You have the option of calling for delivery at any time during the 30 days. Your loss is limited to the prices you pay for the premium, which is the same as buying insurance with a Call. For example:

Suppose a man has a house for sale and agrees to sell it to you for $5,000 and deliver it at that price 60 days later. You pay him $100 for the privilege of buying the house or rejecting it. If at the end of 30 or 60 days you are able to sell the house for $500 profit or for $1000 profit, then you exercise your option to buy the house for $5,000 and sell it to the man so you can make a profit. But if the option expires and you are unable to sell the house for more than the price, then you loose the $100 and do not have to buy the house.

The same applies in buying Calls on a stock. For example: If you buy a Call when Chrysler is selling around 105, good for 30 days at 110, you pay $142.50 which includes the Federal taxes. Suppose before the 30 days are up, Chrysler advances to 115, which would give you a profit of $500, you can sell Chrysler any time it reaches 115 and demand delivery of the stock at 110. But if Chrysler sells at 115 within 10 days after you bought the option and you believe that the trend is up and Chrysler is going higher, then you hold and do not exercise your option or sell the stock. Just before the and of the 30 days, if Chrysler is selling at 120, you could sell 100 shares of Chrysler at 120 and then call for delivery on your Call at 110 making a profit of $1 000, less your commission and the amount paid for the Call. On the other hand, after you have bought the Call at 140, if at no time it advances above 110 and at the end of 30 days Chrysler is selling below 110, you, of course, make no profit and are only out the amount of money that you paid for the Call.

A PUT is an option or an agreement with a man from whom you buy the Put that you can deliver to him the stock at a fixed price any time within 30 days after you buy the Put. A Put costs you $137.50 per 100 shares, We will take this example: When Chrysler is selling at 105, say, you believe it is going down and buy a Put for

30 days at 100, for which you pay $137.30. This means that when Chrysler declines below100, it puts you in a position of being short 100 shares at that price because the man from whom you bought must take from you 100 shares of Chrysler at 100 any time that you deliver it to him within the 30-day period. We will assume that Chrysler goes below 100 and declines to 95. You can buy 100 shares when it goes to 95 and then hold it to the end of the 30 days. In the meantime if Chrysler advances to 105, giving you 10 points profit, you could sell it out. Then at the end of the time the option expired if Chrysler was still selling above 100, you would have made the profit on the stock that you bought against the Put and would simply let the option expire and only be out the price you paid for it. But, on the other hand if you do not trade against the Put and the stock declines and, we will say, at the end of 30 days is selling around 90, you then buy 100 shares of Chrysler and your broker delivers 100 shares to the man that you bought the Put from, giving you the profit

of $1000 less the money you paid for the option and your commission.

PUTS and CALLS are perfectly safe because every Put and Call sold by a reliable Put and call broker is endorsed by a member of the New York Stock Exchange who is thoroughly reliable and will deliver you the stock that he agrees to deliver on which he sold an option or will receive from you any stock that he agrees to buy on an option.

Again, to make it plainer, when you buy a Call on a stock you are long of the market if it goes above the price at which you bought it, just the same as if you had the stock bought, except that your risk is limited. Again, when you buy a Put on a stock, it means that you are short at the price at which you bought the Put, but you do not have to put up any margin or have to stand any loss except the price you paid for the Put. Then as it declines below the price at which you bought the Put, you are making money just the same as if you made a short sale.

SPREAD OR STRADDLE

When you buy a Put and a Call on the same stock it in called a Spread. For example: Suppose Chrysler is selling at 100 and you are in doubt whether it will go up or down but you want to take advantage of a move when it gets under way. Therefore we will say that you buy a Put at 86 and a call at 104. Let us assume that the market starts to react and declines to 95, then hesitates and looks like making bottom. Then you buy 100 shares of Chrysler, knowing that if it continues to decline you cannot lose anything because you have a Put at 96. Let us assume that you are right and the market starts to advance. It continues to advance and before the end of the 30 days Chrysler advances to 110 and there are 6 points' profit in the Call that you bought at 104. You also still have the stock that you bought against the Put at 96. Now, you can sell out 200 shares of stock and call for the 100 shares at 104, which gives you a profit on the Call and your Put expires because it is of no value.

Often Spreads can be bought very close to the market when you are buying a Put and a Call from the same man. On some stocks you can often buy Spreads at the market by paying an additional premium. As a rule it would not pay to buy a Spread except on very active stocks which have a very wide fluctuation during the 30 days, giving you a chance to operate against both the Put and the Call during the month. At least when you buy a Spread if the stock moves 10 or 15 points or more in either direction, you are sure to make some money. However, it is not always advisable to spend as much as it costs to buy Spreads unless the market looks like it is going to be very active and you are trading in high-priced stocks.

Put and Call brokers give these definitions: "A PUT is a negotiable contract by which the taker may put to the maker a certain lot of securities at a specified price on/or before a fixed date. A CALL is the opposite. A SPREAD is one PUT and one CALL. PREMIUM is the money paid for a PUT, CALL or SPEAD. MAKER is he who writes or sells PUTS, CALLS and SPREADS. ENDORSER is a N.Y. Stock Exchange firm which guarantees, PUT, CALL or SPREA.D contract by endorsing it like a check. The insurance feature provided by these privileges is considered valuable.

HOW PUTS AND CALLS ARE SOLD

Puts and Calls are sold by traders and large operators who make it a business trading in and out of the market and selling Puts or Calls on the stocks that they have bought or sold, but Puts and Calls are always endorsed by members of the New York Stock Exchange. As a rule, Puts and Calls are sold so many points away from the market; that is, a call costs you $142.50 and the price that it is away from the market depends upon the activity of the stock and the condition of the market. A Put is the reverse, so many points below the price at which the market is selling that day, depending upon the price of the stack and the activity of the market. However often traders who make it a business of selling Puts and Calls, sell them at the market price for an additional premium. For example, Douglas Aircraft might be selling at 56 and by paying a premium $300 to the seller you could buy a Call or a Put on Doug for 30 days at 56, therefore when it moved 3 points up or down from the price at which you bought the Call or the Put, you would have made the money back or the price of the stock would show you a profit for the money you paid out; then when it went more than 3 points in your favor, you would have a net profit above the price you paid for the privilege, either Put or Call that you bought at the market.

As a rule, I favor buying Puts and Calls with risk limited to the price of $142.50 per 100 shares for a Call or $137.50 per 100 shares for a Put, and buying Puts or Calls a number of points away from the price at which the stock is selling.

WHY PUTS AND CALLS ARE SOLD

The question might be asked: If there is a chance to make large profits on a small risk in buying Puts and Calls, why do traders and wealthy speculators sell them?

Often a trader who is out of the market is willing to buy stocks if they decline 4 or 5 points, therefore he will sell you a Put on a stock 3 or 5 Points away and you pay him the premium of $137.50; then if the stock declines to the level at which he is willing to buy and even though it goes lower, you deliver it to him, he is satisfied to buy it at that level. On the other hand, often these big traders have accumulated a large line of stock and already have profits in them, so they are willing to sell all or part of their line should the market advance 5 or 10 points more, therefore they are willing to sell you

Calls on the stocks they hold or part of what they hold 5 or 10 points above the market, as the case may be, and are perfectly willing to deliver you the stock and permit you to have the profit above that price for the premium that you pay. Another reason they sell them is that they know they can always protect themselves. If the market is very strong and you are going to make profits on the Call they sold to you or you are going to call the stock, they can buy more. On the other hand, suppose they sell you Puts: The market starts declining fast and looks like going lower, where you will have a profit on the Put you bought, they can sell short, put up the margin and carry the stock until you deliver it to them against the Put. It is a perfectly legitimate business just the same as insurance business and is fair to both buyer and seller.

LENGTH OF TIME PUTS AND CALLS ARE SOLD

As a rule, you can buy Puts and Calls good 7 days, two weeks, and 30 days, and sometimes you can buy them good 60 or 90 days, but most traders who make it a business of selling Puts and Calls do not write them for more than 30 days. However, you can always ask your broker or the Put and Call broker to make an inquiry and get you a quote on what you can buy Puts and Calls for good 30, 60 or 90 days; then if the price looks right, you can buy them.

My advice is that you will make more money buying Puts and Calls good 30 days than you will buying them good 7 days or two weeks because the shorter periods of time, except when markets are extremely active, do not give you an opportunity for a wide enough range to make profits. However, when you buy Puts or Calls good 7 days or 14 days you pay less premium than for those good 30 days. The premium, as a rule, for 7 days is $62.50; two weeks is $87.50.

HOW TO BUY PUTS AND CALLS

If you live outside New York City, you can give an order to your local broker and he will buy Puts and Calls for your account that are endorsed by a New York Stock Exchange firm and place them to your credit with your broker in New York City or the correspondent of the house you trade with in your capital city. Then when you want to make a trade against your Puts or Calls, or want, to buy or sell and call the stock or put it and take profits, the broker will take care of the transaction for you. Always deal with brokers who are members of the New York Stock Exchange when you buy or sell stocks.

The unit for Puts and Calls is 100 shares, but at times you may be able to buy odd-lots or 50-share lots of Puts and Calls; but when you buy Puts or Calls be sure that they are endorsed by a New York Stock Exchange firm. There are often bucket shops that will sell you Puts and Calls on 10 shares, 25 shares or anything else, but there is no Stock Exchange firm behind them, and you have no assurance of getting your profit if you make them.

PUT AND CALL BROKERS

There are many brokers in Puts and Calls in New York City who buy and sell Puts and Calls for a commission and have the Puts and Calls endorsed by a New York Stock Exchange house and deliver them to you or to your broker. Any honest broker can stand investigation and for your own protection you should ascertain whether the Put and Call broker whom you buy Puts and Calls from is reliable and will have the Puts and Calls guaranteed by a firm that is a member of the Now York Stock Exchange.

ADVANTAGE OF BUYING PUTS AND CALLS DIRECT

Should you want to send orders direct to buy Puts and Calls, you can send your check or money order direct to a Put and Call broker in New York and he will buy Puts and Calls for your account on your order and mail them direct to you or deliver them to your bank or your broker, as you request.

The advantage in sending your order direct to a Put and Call broker instead of over a broker's private wire is that you often get quicker service by using the Postal Telegraph or Western Union because all orders over brokers' private wires to buy and sell stocks have precedence over all messages pertaining to off the-floor business. This would naturally delay the transmission of your order to buy a Put or Call and if the market is very active, it might result in a point or more against you, whereas if your order went direct to the Put and Call broker by Western Union or Postal Telegraph, you would get a quicker execution. For example: Suppose you decided to buy a Put on Chrysler and you wanted to got it in a hurry; if you sent your order to a Put and Call broker, your telegram would read as follows:

BUY A PUT 100 CHRYSLER CLOSEST OBTAINABLE 30 DAYS

On receipt of this order the Put and Call broker would immediately buy a Put on Chrysler to the best advantage and would wire you the price at which he bought it. You, of course, would have to have your money on deposit with the Put and Call broker before you sent the order because he will not fill orders until the money is in hand. However, you could wire the money with your telegram. You would wire him $137.50 with the above message. On the other hand, if you wanted to buy a Call on Chrysler, then your order would read as follows:

BUY A CALL 100 CHRYSLER CLOSEST OBTATAINABLE 30 DAYS

And with this message to buy a Call, if you did not have the money on deposit with the broker, you would wire $142,50 to pay for the Call.

If you were not in a hurry, you could send a telegram to the Put and Call broker and ask him to quote you Puts and Calls on Chrysler, General Motors, U.S. Steel or any other stocks, good 30 days. He would then wire the price at which he could buy, this price being subject to change any hour or any minute. After receiving the telegram from him, if you thought the price was close enough to the market that you could make money in 30 days, you could then wire your order to buy.

THE ADVANTAGES OF PUTS AND CALLS TO THE BUYER

The great advantage to the man who buys Puts and Calls is that his risk is always limited. Another advantage is that he saves payment of interest. For instance, if you buy a Call and the stock moves up in your favor, for 30 days you do not have to pay any interest until you have called the stock and it has been delivered into your account.

Since the Securities Exchange Commission has raised margin requirements to where it requires 55% margin to buy stocks, it makes it a great advantage to buy Puts and Calls. For example: If you wanted to buy 100 shares of stock selling at $100 per share, you would have to put up $5,500 margin and would expect it to go up more than 5 points if you bought it, therefore instead of putting up $5,500 to buy the stock and carry it and besides pay interest, you buy a Call, we will say, 5 points away for 30 days, which costs you $142.50. Then if the stock advances during the 30 day-period to where you have a profit of $1,000, you have made nearly 100% on your money, On the other hand, if you put up $5,500 and the stock advances so you have a profit of $1,000, your net return on your capital would be less than 20%, while at the same time if you bought 100 shares of stock, on margin, it might decline 10 or 20 points and your loss would be 10 or 20 points according to whether you held it or used a stop loss order and limited your risk.

HOW TO USE PUTS AND CALLS IN PLACE OF STOP LOSS ORDERS

Another advantage in buying Puts and Calls is to protect the stock that you already have bought or to protect the stock that you are already short of. When markets are very wild and active and unexpected events take place that cause stocks to open up or down several points, as has happened many times in the past and will happen again in the future, you want to be protected against losses. You can always use a stop loss order, but if the stock should open off 3, 4, or 5 points under your stop loss order, then your stock will be sold at the market. On the other hand, if you had 100 shares of Chrysler bought at 100 and it declined and closed some night at 97 and you had a stop loss order at 95 and something unexpected happened overnight and the next morning the stock opened at 90, your stock would be sold on stop at 90 at the market and you would lose 5 points more than you expected to lose by placing a stop loss order. If instead of placing a stop loss order when Chrysler was selling around 100, you bought a Put at 95, than when the stock opened off at 90 and continued to 80, your stock would be protected at 95 or you could deliver it at 95 on the Put and would not lose anything by the overnight drop, the Put having protected you against the unexpected.

Reverse the position. Suppose you are short of Chrysler at 100 and have a stop loss order on it at 105. If the unexpected happened and Chrysler opened at 110, then your stop loss order would be executed 5 points higher than you expected and you would lose $500 or 5 points more than you had figured on. On the other hand, if you had a Call bought on

Chrysler to protect your short sale and Chrysler opened 5 points above your stop loss order some morning, then the Call would protect you because you would have a contract to buy the stock at a price on the Call; and you could call it and deliver it against your short sale.

Thus, you see that you can use Puts or Calls for insurance or for protection when you are long or short of the market, just the same as you use them to limit your risk in getting in and out of the market, limiting your loss to the amount you pay for a Put or a Call when you want to take advantage of a Stock that you think may have a fast move one way or the other.

WHEN TO BUY PUTS AND CALLS

The time to buy to buy Puts and Calls is when stocks are very active or just before activity starts. You can determine when to buy Puts and Calls and on what stocks to buy Puts Or Calls by reading, studying and applying the rules in my books—*Truth of the Stock Tape, Wall Street Stock Selector*, and *New York Stock Trend Detector*.

I will give you a few rules that will help you to determine the time to buy Puts or Calls:

RULE 1: Buy Calls around double bottoms or triple bottoms, or buy the stock around double or triple bottoms; and buy Puts, which will protect you should the stock break the old bottom. By this I mean, if a stock has held at a low level, then advances, then reacts to that same low level months later and makes a bottom, this would be a double bottom. Then if it advances and reacts the third time to around the same level, this would be a triple bottom.

Reverse this rule at tops. Buy Puts around double or triple tops, or sell the stock short, and buy Calls for protection in case the stock should cross the old tops.

It is always well even when stocks are moving very fast and are very active to wait several weeks or several months if a stock holds around a bottom or top before you buy Calls or Puts, giving the stock time to complete accumulation or distribution because this has to take place before there is a reverse move of a large number of points. You can easily see this by a study of past action of stocks on charts.

RULE 2: Buy Calls when old levels are crossed. If a stock stays for several weeks, several months, or even several years in a narrow trading range around top levels, as referred to in my books, then when it breaks over the previous tops, it certainly will indicate activity. That is the time to buy a Call, as I will prove in examples later. Reverse this rule. When a stocks holds for a long around low levels, then breaks the first support point, buy Puts or sell the stock short and buy Calls for protection.

RULE 3: If a stock advances to a top that it has made many months previous or many years previous and fails to go thru, then has a reaction; then rallies and makes a lower top, that is, a third top and fails to go thru, this would be the place to sell the stock short and buy a call for protection in case the stock went higher. It would also be the place to buy a Put for 30 days, because if this top is a final top and the stock is starting on a long decline, you would make money on the Put and could also be short of the stock at the same time by putting up margin.

Reverse this rule after a prolonged decline. If a stock makes a second or third higher bottom several weeks or months apart, then shows activity on the upside, it is the time to buy Calls or buy the stock and buy Puts for protection.

RULE 4: When a stock holds for several months around the same level and fails to break the first support point, buy a Put and buy the stock when it begins to show activity, or buy a Call as soon as activity starts on the upside. (See example of Chrysler February 3, 1936 to June 5, 1936)

Reverse this rule when a stock holds for several months around top levels and fails to cross the first top. Buy a Put when activity starts an the down side or buy a Call and to go short.

RULE 5: After a stock advances thru an old top where it has held for several weeks or several months, and advances several points above this top, then reacts to the old top, buy Puts and buy the stock, or buy Calls.

Reverse this rule in a bear market. When a stock breaks thru an old bottom and goes several points below it, then rallies back to the old bottom, buy Calls and sell short against them, or buy Puts.

RULE 6: In a Bull market, when trend is up, wait for reaction of 5, 10 or 12 points, then buy Calls, or buy the stock and buy Puts to protect the purchase.

In a Bear Market, wait for rallies of 5, 7, 10 or 12 points, then buy Puts, or sell short and buy Calls to protect the trade.

RULE 7: Buy a Call when a stock reacts 40 to 50% of the last advance or buy the stock and buy Puts to protect it.

Reverse this rule in bear market: Buy Puts when a stock rallies 40 to 50% of last move or buy Calls when it rallies to protect short sales. For example: Suppose a stock advances from 100 to 120. A decline to 110 would be one-half or 50% of the advance. If all indications point to a bear market with the main trend down, then you would buy Puts when the stock rallied 40 to 50%. Example: U. S. Steel, March 6 to 11, 1937, made top at 126½. After an advance of over 50 points, a big reaction could be expected and it was time to buy Put. March 22, U. S. Steel declined to 112½, down 14 points from the top. A 50% rally would be 7 points or to 119½, where you would buy Puts. Steel advances to on 123½, on March 31, better than 50%, giving a good opportunity to buy Puts for 30 days, which made good, as Steel declined 24 points in 30 days.

WHEN TO BUY MORE PUTS AND CALLS ON THE SAME STOCK

Suppose a stock breaks out on the upside, moves up fast and shows up trend. You have bought Calls and have profits in the first month. The trend still shows up and when it crosses previous tops or Resistance Levels, then you buy Calls the next month and can protect what profits you have on the first Calls by buying Puts under the market and still carry your original stock.

Many traders do this when a move of 50 or 60 points takes place in two or three months. They continue to buy Calls every month and continue to carry their stock and then often buy Puts to protect their profits instead of placing stop loss orders, thus making a large amount of profit on a very small risk.

HOW TO TRADE AGAINST PUTS AND CALLS

Suppose you buy a Call on General Motors at 50. At the time you buy the Gall General Motors is selling at 47. You have bought a Call at 50, good 30 days. When General Motors advances to 50, holds for several days and doesn't look like going thru, you could then sell short 50 shares of General Motors; then no matter which way General Motors went, up or down, you would make money. If it advanced to 55, you would still have a profit of 5 points on your Call, and on the stock that you sold short at 50, you would have a loss of 5 points, but this would be made up because you could call 100 shares. After you sold short at 50, if you were right and General Motors declined to 45 or to 40, then when your Call expired it would be of no value but the stock that you sold short would be down a 5 points or more and you could close your short trade with a profit.

Example of trading against a Put: Suppose Douglas Aircraft is selling around 50 and you buy a Put on 100 shares, good 30 days, at 46. Douglas declines to 46 or to 45 and holds for several days and looks like making bottom and not going any lower, but you are not certain which way it will go for the remainder of the time for which your Put is good, so you buy 50 shares of Douglas at 46 against your Put; then if it goes up 5 points you are making profit on the stock you bought and you cannot lose because you have a Put. Then, if it should decline 5 points, you could have a profit of 5 points on your Put and could deliver 100 shares against what you bought and have no loss except the cost of the commission and the premium paid for your Put.

Many shrewd traders who buy Puts and Calls make money trading against them, and at the end of the time the Put or Call expires there is no profit in it but they have made a profit because they traded on the fluctuations of the market. Often you can sell against a Put or buy against a Call, several times during the month and scalp anywhere from 2 to 5 points or more and possibly make 10 points' profit and be protected all the time and yet at the end of the Put there would be no profit in it.

Some traders handle Puts and Calls in this way: Suppose they have bought a Call on a stock at 100 and it advances to 110; then they buy a Call for 30 days longer at a higher level, and when the first Call expires on which they have profit, they call the stock in and do not sell it out; then buy a Put to protect their profit and continue to buy Calls and buy Puts, pyramiding all the way up, not selling out their stock until they think the time has come for a change in the main trend.

This way of trading is reversed on the downside of the market. Buying a Put and getting short, buying more Puts an the way down; staying short; then buying a Call to protect the short stock, following the main trend for several months or as long as it indicates that it is down.

KIND OF STOCKS TO BUY PUTS AND CALLS ON

Stocks always move faster at higher levels than they do at low levels, therefore, as a general rule, you can make the most money by buying Puts and Calls on stocks selling between $75 and $150 per share, but there are times when you buy Calls on stocks selling between $5 and $10 and make a large percentage on the risk.

The next range of price is between $20 and $36. In this range you can often buy Puts and Calls at the market or within one or two points of the price at which the stock is selling.

After stocks cross $36 to $40 per share they move much faster, therefore you will make more money by buying in the same way; by buying Calls or Puts on stocks selling at 100 or higher you will make more money as they will decline faster until they get down to around 50 to 40; then in most cases they will decline slower. Therefore your chance of making profits are less in buying Puts or Calls on lower-priced stocks. I will give examples later and you can see by watching and studying charts when there are often opportunities for very large profits when a low-priced stock gets out of the zone of accumulation. In the same way, when a stock is in a congested area at high levels and remains in a narrow trading range for a long time, then breaks out, you can then make money buying Puts just as big decline is ready to start.

EXAMPLES OF TRADING WITH PUTS AND CALLS

CHRYSLER MOTORS

1932 - July 30, note Chrysler on the Weekly Chart had remained in a narrow trading range for 8 weeks after it had made bottom at 5. When it crossed 8 it was over the top of the previous weeks and indicated higher. At that time you could probably have bought a Call on Chrysler around 10. It advanced to 16 in 30 days and was up to 21¾ in 6 weeks, giving a possible profit of 10 to 12 points. This trade would have been made by watching the chart and seeing a long period of congestion in a narrow trading range and then not anticipating anything but waiting until the stock showed itself by advancing above the tops of the previous weeks; then you would buy the Call.

1933 - April 25, again Chrysler crossed 8 weeks tops. You could probably have bought a Call at this time around 15 good for 30 days. It advanced to 21½ and the trend did not turn down, the stock continuing up until it reached 39½, showing a possible profit of around 24 points. After the stock advanced to where you had a profit of 10 points or more, you could have bought a Put which would protected the profits, or followed it up with a stop loss order after you had called the stock which you bought lower.

1934 - February 3 to March 1, Chrysler made tops around 60, showing that it was meeting great resistance. Around March 1st you could probably have bought a Put at 55. The stock started a downward move and declined to 49 in 30 days; then rallied to 56 and you could probably have bought a Call around 55 before the rally took place, which would have protected your short sales; then you could have stayed short. The stock declined on May 19 to 36½, then rallied to 44 and continued on down to 29¼ on August 7, giving another possibility for a profit of 20 to 25 points on Puts and a limited risk of not more than $280 if you bought a Put and then bought a Call, after it went down, to protect your profits.

1935 - March 12, Chrysler reached a low of 31. It had made bottom at 29¼ in August 1934, and made a double bottom at 29⅜ in September 1934. This decline to 31 was a third bottom at a higher level and would have been a place at which to buy the stock with a stop under 29¼ or to buy Calls because this was a double and triple bottom. Around that time you could probably have bought a Call around 34 or 35 because the stock had been narrow for a long. In 4 weeks it had advanced to 37 and the trend continued up until May 25, when it reached 49½, giving an opportunity far a profit of at least 10 points net. Then the stock reacted to 41½, which was an old top and a place to again buy a Call or to buy a Put and trade against it.

In July and August 1935, Chrysler crossed 60, the old top of 1934, and held for 4 weeks without breaking back under 57, which according to the rules in my books, was a place to buy with stop at 57. Having crossed top of 1934, it indicated higher. After holding for 4 weeks in a narrow trading range, around September 10 you could probably have bought a Call at 65. In 30 days it was up to 74½, the main trend strong up. You could have bought another Call and also bought a Put and held your stock after calling at the time the first option expired.

In November 1935, Chrysler advanced to 90 and at no time had it reacted 5 points after it crossed 60. This was another opportunity for make 25 to 30 points' net profit on an original risk of $142.50 and you might have bought more Calls on the way up after you had profits and started handling a pyramid and made much larger profits.

Always watch a stock if it makes a top or a bottom and holds for several months without making the first support level; then when it begins to show activity by breaking to new lows or advancing to new highs, it is the time to buy a Put or a Call. (Refer to Rule 4)

1936 - February 3, Chrysler declined about 10 points, making low at 91½; then advanced on April 13 to 103⅞; then again declined on April 30 to 91⅝ and held in this range until June 5, when again it was down to 91⅝. From February to early June, nearly 5 months, it held in a narrow range without breaking the low level of 91½, and making bottom for so many months around this level indicated that it due for a big move one way or the other. In the early part of June you could probably have bought a Call on Chrysler around 97, good 30 days, but if you waited until it crossed several weeks' tops at 98, you would have bought a Call in the early part of July good 30 days, which you could probably have bought around 100 to 101. In 30 days it was up to 116, when you would have a profit of 12 to 16 points. It went right on up to 124⅞ on July 27, advancing 32 points from the low of June 5 without ever reacting 5 points. If you had bought stock when it was near the low or bought a Call, you could have called the stock; then bought a Put to protect it and kept it right on thru, or you could have put a stop loss order on it and carried it thru. In the second month you could have bought another Call. This move certainly gave you an opportunity to make 25 points or more on a Call.

After a sharp advance of 32 points in less than two months, you could naturally expect a reaction. After these fast moves, as a General rule, the reaction runs one half of 50%. (See rule 7) When Chrysler was around 124, you could probably have bought a Put at 119 to 117. On August 21 Chrysler declined to 108⅝, down 16 points, giving you a chance to make profit of 6 to 7 points, anyway, on a Put. Then it held for 5 weeks between 108⅝ and 117; then started up. When it started up you could have again bought a Call. It advanced 18 points in 30 days, advancing to 130½, affording another excellent opportunity for profits on Calls.

On November 12, 1936, Chrysler made the high of its move at 138¾. This was an important point because the top made on October 6, 1926 was 140½. You would sell out long stock around these levels and go short with a stop above 140½. This was also the level at which to buy Puts or Calls. You could buy Calls and then go short or buy Puts expecting that it would not go to a new high. You could probably have bought a Put at 130 or higher. In 30 days Chrysler was down to 121; then continued down to 110¾, which price it reached on January 4, 1537, down 28 points. You certainly would have an opportunity on this decline to make 15 or 20 points on Puts, or after you bought the first Put and it declined, you could have bought a Call for protection and carried the stock on down.

1937 - Around January 4 would be a time to buy a Call or a Put because the stock was down near the low levels of 108⅝ made on August 21, 1936. You could have bought a Put at this time and then bought the stock, figuring that it would not break the old low levels before a good rally, or when it reached 110¾ or anywhere around that level, you could have bought a Call, probably at 117, good 30 days. Before the 30 days was up Chrysler was up to 124, and on February 11 advanced to 135¼ giving a possible profit of 15 points. This would be another place to buy a Call and go short figuring the stock would not cross the old top at 138¾, or after you saw it hold and not go thru, you could buy a Put. Chrysler first declined to 124; then rallied to 234⅞ on March 3. This was the third top around the same level, 135¼ being a lower top than 138¾, and 134⅞ being slightly lower than the other top. This was an excellent time to go short of the stock with a stop above old tops and also a good time to buy Puts because the old tops were so close.

It declined in 30 days to 120; then you would have bought a Call to protect your profits on the Put and could have bought another Put good 30 days. By May 13 the stock declined to 106½, down 29 points from the top, giving an opportunity for a profit of 20 points or more on Puts. Then Chrysler rallied on May 24 to 115, a rally of 8½ points, which was a fair sized rally in a weak market. On May 24, when Chrysler was selling around 114⅝, Puts were offered at 110, good for 30 days at a cost of $137.50.

U.S. STEEL

We will give you some examples as to where Puts and Calls could have been bought on U. S. STEEL to advantage:

1932 - May 7 to June 28, high and low on U. S. Steel during this period was 31½ and 21¼. When Steel declined to around 22 you could buy Calls because the low of 1927 was at 21⅞. You could probably have bought a Call at that time at 25 or lower, or you could have bought a Put and bought the stock against it. Another way to trade would have been to wait until U. S. Steel crossed the top of 32, which was above 7 or 8 weeks' tops, then bought Calls. In 30 days it advanced to 44 and by September 6 advanced to 52½, giving a possible profit of 25 to 30 points on Calls.

1933 - July 18, U. S. Steel advanced to 67½ and by July 21 declined to 49, down 18 points in three days. A Put good 7 days or two weeks at that time would have made good. However, when it was around the high levels, if you had bought a Put good 30 days, you could have made profits because the stock declined again to 49 on August 16 and never rallied above 58 until it declined to 34¾ on October 21, 1933.

1935 -- January 8, U. S. Steel made high at 40, March 18 declined to 27½. This would have been a place to buy Puts or Calls because it was a double bottom against a low made September 17, 1934, when Steel sold at 29¼. You could have bought the stock and bought Puts as protection, or you could have bought Calls, or you could have waited until after U. S. Steel crossed 40, the high of January, and then bought Calls. After it crossed 40, it never sold at 40 again until it advanced to 72 on April 9, 1936. Thus, you can see that if you had bought stock and bought Puts or bought Calls and once had profits in them, you could have moved up the stop loss order to protect the profits and carried it for big profits.

1936 – April - You could probably bought Puts on U. S. Steel good 30 days around 66. Within 30 days it declined to 54¼, giving an opportunity to make a profit of 10 to 12 points in 30 days.

October 3 to January 9, 1937, U. S. Steel held in a range from 72 to 80, or four months in an 8-point range. When Steel narrows down for several months like this, it is getting ready for a big move one way or the other.

On November 23 when it declined to 72, it was at the old top of April 9, 1936, a buying point, or a place to buy Puts and buy the stock, or to buy Calls, but a better time and the surest place to buy Calls was when it crossed 80 on January 7, 1937. You could probably have bought Calls at that time at 85 good for 30 days. The last low was made at 79 on January 12 and in 30 days or February 11 U. S. Steel sold at 109½, giving a possible profit of 24 points. With the 15 Trend still up you could probably have bought Puts at 5 points down to protect your profit and hold your stock. You could also have bought Calls good 30 days.

1937 - March 11, U.S. Steel advanced to 129½, up 57½ points in 60 days. Thus, after the long period of dullness in an 8-point range, you had an opportunity in 60 days to make profits of over 50 points by buying calls. Then, after this rapid advance you could have bought a Put. On March 22 U.S. Steel declined to 123 ½, lower than the first top. This would have been the time to buy Calls and go short because it was near the old top, or to buy Puts. You could probably have bought Puts at this time around 117. Thirty days later U.S. Steel was down to 99. Then, if you were short on Puts, you could have bought a Call to protect your profits or placed a stop loss order to protect your profits. On May 18 U.S. Steel declined to 91⅝, down 32 points in 48 days. This shows you that when activity follows a long period of dullness there are big opportunities for making large profits on small risks in Puts and Calls.

RULES FOR BUYING PUTS AND CALLS ON LOW PRICED STOCKS

Many low priced stocks remain in a narrow trading range for many years and do not offer any opportunity for making profits buying Puts and Calls. Therefore, if you bought too often without waiting for definite indications on low priced stocks, you would just lose the money you paid out for Puts and Calls.

You must have a rule to determine when to buy Puts and Calls on low priced stocks because at times there are really big opportunities for making profits if you study and watch stocks when they start to move from low levels. You either have to wait until stock holds in a narrow trading range from 4 to 6 months or until it holds in a narrow trading range for several years and then crosses the old top levels and shows activity; that is when you can buy Calls. For example:

JOHNS MANVILLE

1929 – February, Johns Manville advanced to a high of 242. There is no use talking about how much money could have been made buying Puts even 20, 30 or 50 points away on high priced stocks in 1929 or buying Puts to protect stocks that people were long of. The opportunities were certainly there. But I want be conservative and point out how profits can be made trading in Puts and Calls in normal markets.

1932 - During April, May, June and July Johns Manville made a low month at 10 and the high during that period was 16. It started up around the middle of July 1932, after the general market had made bottom. Of course, after it stayed several months around 10, you could have bought a Put probably one point down and could have bought the stock, but the safest and best time was in August when it crossed 16; then you could probably have bought a Call at 19 or 20. It was then above a four-months' range and showed that it was going to move up. In 30 days it advanced to 29 and in the early part of September sold at 33. There was certainly an opportunity to make 10 to 12 points' profit buying Calls on a low priced stock after it gave a signal to advance.

1933 - March, Johns Manville declined to 13, 3 points above the old low level of 1932 and a place to buy with a stop under 10 a or a place to buy Puts and buy the stock; also a place to buy Calls.

In May the stock crossed 33, the high of September 1932, which indicated activity and higher prices. You could have bought a Call after it crossed 33, which would have made you at least 15 points' profit in 30 days. In July Johns Manville sold at 60.

1935 - In July Johns Manville crossed a series of tops at 57. This was the time to buy Calls. In August 1935, it crossed 67, the top of February, 1934, another time to buy Calls because it indicated a definite trend up. It never reacted over 10 points until it sold at 129 in February 1936. You could have bought Calls right along all the way up or bought Puts to protect your profits on Calls and made large profits.

BOEING AIRCRAFT

September 1934, to July 1935, this stock had a range between 11¼ and 6¼, or a range of 5 points. From March 1935 to June 1935, it moved in a range of 2 points between 6¼ and 8¼. In July 1935, it advanced to 9, crossing the tops of the previous three months. This was a place to buy Calls. However, if you had waited until it crossed 12 in August and bought Calls when it was above all these, you could have made big profits because it never sold below 12 until it advanced to 26½ in January 1936. Notice how much faster the stock moved up after it reached high levels. I have told you that when stocks get above 36 to 40, they move much faster. In March 1937, Boeing advanced to 49½, up 13 points in 13 days.

DOUGLAS AIRCRAFT

1935 - March, low 17½; October and November, high 35; December, low 34. Then it crossed the old high levels and advanced to 59 in the same month, making a range of 25 points, the first month after it got above 36. Of course, there was big money in buying Calls good for 30 days.

1936 – January, Douglas made a low of 50½ and the same month advanced to 75½, making a 25 point range in 30 days, again proving how much faster stocks move after they get above 50 and the greater opportunities for profits as they move into higher levels.

Bottom at 29¼ in August 1934, and made a double bottom at 29⅜ September 1934. This decline to 31 was a third bottom at a higher level and would have been a place at which to buy the stock with a stop under 29¼ or to buy Calls because this was a double and triple bottom. Around that time you could probably have bought a Call around 34 or 35 because the stock had been narrow for a long time. In 4 weeks it advanced to 37 and the trend continued up until May 25, when it reached 49½, giving an opportunity for a profit of at least 10 points net. Then the stock reacted to 41½, which was an old top and a place to again buy a Call or to buy a Put and trade against it.

In July and August 1935, Chrysler crossed 60, the old top of 1934, and held for 4 weeks without breaking back under 57, which according to the rules in my books, was a place to buy with a stop at 57. Having crossed the top of 1934, it indicated higher. After holding for 4 weeks in a narrow trading range, around September 10 you could probably have bought a Call at 65. In 30 days it was up to 74½ with the main tread strong up. You could have bought another Call and also bought a Put and held your stock after calling it at the time the first option expired.

In November 1935, Chrysler advanced to 90 and at no time had it reacted 5 points after it crossed 60. This was another opportunity for making 25 to 30 points' net profit on an original risk of $142.50 and you might even have bought more Calls on the way up after you had profits and started handling a pyramid and made much larger profits.

Always watch a stock if it makes a top or a bottom and holds for several months without breaking the first support level; then when it begins to show activity by breaking to new lows or advancing to new highs, it is the time to buy a Put or a Call. (Refer to Rule 4)

1936 - February 3, Chrysler declined about
10 points, making low at 91½, then advanced
on April 13 to 103⅞; then again declined on
April 30 to 91⅝ and held in this range until
June 5, when it was again down to 91⅝.
From February to early June, nearly 5
months, it held in a narrow range without
breaking the low level of 91½, and making
bottom for so many months around this level
indicated that it was due for a big move one
way or the other. In the early part of June
you could probably have bought a Call on
Chrysler around 97, good 30 days, but if you
waited until it crossed several weeks tops at
98, you would have bought a Call in the early
part of July good 30 days, which you could
probably have bought around 100 to 101. In
30 days it was up to 116, when you would
have a profit of 12 to 16 points. It went right
on up to 124⅞ on July 27, advancing 32
points from the low of June 5 without ever
reacting 5 points. If you had bought stock

when it was near the low or bought a Call, you could have called the stock; then bought a Put to protect it, and kept it right on thru, or you could have put a stop loss order on it and carried it thru. In the 18 November, 1936, Douglas high 77; December high 77¾.

1937 - January, high 77. Three months with tops around the same level. This would have been a time to buy Calls and go short because the high level of the stock was 82, made in October 1936. It was also a time to buy Puts because they could probably have been bought 5 points down or you could have waited until the stock broke 68, the low of December 1936, and then bought Puts good 30 days. The stock declined fast and after you had profits on Puts, you could have bought a Call and carried it on down.

In May 1937, Douglas declined to 47½, down

30 points from the January high, affording excellent opportunities for pyramiding on the way down and selling the stock short or for staying short after you once had a profit in a Put and a chance to protect it with a call. The percentage of profits compared to the risk would have been enormous.

The above examples show you the advantages and opportunities of using Puts and Calls at critical times and when stocks are active. No one can expect to make a great success in any line of business unless they study it constantly and learn more and more about it. There is no business in the world that will return greater profit on the risk and the capital than speculation, using Puts and Calls, provided you keep up monthly and weekly high and low charts on quite a few stocks and study them. Follow the rules laid down in my books, *Truth of the Stock Tape,* *Wall Street Stock Selector,* and *New York Stock Trend Detector,* and you will learn how to trade successfully in Puts and Calls.

The more you study the market and the more you study Puts and Calls and learn how to operate, the more advantages you will see in using them.

—W. D. GANN

HOW TO SELL

PUTS AND CALLS

Many people know how to buy Puts and Calls but very few know how to sell them or know that they can sell them and get the premium money for the Option.

When you sell a Put or a Call on stocks, you are simply taking the opposite position to the one when you buy a Put or a Call and there are more advantages on the selling side, especially at certain periods of the market.

Suppose you wish to buy U.S. Steel. Naturally, you want to get in the market and buy at the lowest level possible, but you cannot be sure of the exact bottom. For example: We will assume that U.S. Steel is selling at 66, and you feel that you would be willing to buy it if it declines to around 62. You have your account open with your broker and your money on deposit to cover the margin requirements to buy U.S. Steel. You give your broker an order to sell a Put on 100 U.S. Steel good 30 days - which is always below the market, varying from 2 to 3 points to as much as 10 to 15 points. We will assume that the broker sells the Put on U.S. Steel at 62, good 30 days, and receives $112.50, which is credited to your account. This is the premium that you receive from the buyer. Then, we will assume that U.S. Steel does not decline to 62 before the 30-day Put expires. Therefore, you will have the $112.50 which you received for the Put.

Then, if you are still willing and want to buy U.S. Steel, you could sell another Put an 100 shares, good for 30 days, at whatever number of points below the market the broker could get it. In this case, we will assume that Steel is selling around 63 and the broker sells the Put for you at 59, again receiving $112.50 credited to your account. Then suppose U.5. Steel declines to 58 and closes at the end of 30 days at 58. The man who bought from you the Put on 100 U.S. Steel at 59 will put it to you or deliver it to your broker for 59 and you will have bought Steel at 59 and will have $250.00 to your credit, the money you received on the Puts sold.

Then, we will assume that you are willing to take 4 or 5 points profit on U.S. Steel. You give your broker an order to sell a Call on U.S. Steel good 30 days. We will assume he sells it at 64 and again you receive $112.50 premium. If at the end of the 30 days U.S. Steel has not reached 64, you still have the stock and have $375.00 to your credit, which you have received for selling Puts and Calls.

We will assume that at the end of the 30 days U.S Steel is selling at 63. You instruct your broker to sell a Call on U.S. Steel good 30 days, and he sells it at 67 and receives $112.50 for your account. At the end of the 30 days, or when the Call expires, U.S. Steel is selling at 69 and the man to whom you sold the Call demands delivery; then your broker delivers 100 U.S. Steel For 67. You have sold at 67 the Steel that you bought at 59 and have made 8 points profit or $800.00, less commission and interest, and you have received $450.00 premium money for the Puts and Calls you sold, which is just that much extra profit because you did not take as much risk as you would if you had just bought U. S. Steel or sold it without selling the Puts or Calls.

SELLING CALLS TO GET SHORT OF THE MARKET

Suppose you think the market is about high enough to sell short but you are not sure just when and where the top will be reached. U.S. Steel is selling around 75 when you make up your mind to sell it short. Then you give your broker an order to sell a Call on 100 U.S. Steel good 30 days. He sells the Call at 80 which means that if U.S. Steel is selling above 80 at the end of 30 days, the man you sold the option to will call it or buy it from you at 80 and you will be short at 80 with a credit of $112.50 which you received for the Call.

You might be able to sell Calls twice, three times, five times or more and take in the premium money before the stock is called. Suppose, after you have been called for Steel at 80, which puts you short at 80, you decide to sell a Put. You get it at 75, which gives you 5 points profit, and you again receive $112.50 for the Put good 30 days. We will assume that at the end of 30 days Steel is selling at 74 and the man you sold the Put to, delivers 100 shares of Steel to the broker for your account. This means that you have bought 100 shares at 75 and covered your short position, making a profit of 5 points or $500.00 less commission and taxes; and at the same time you have made $225.00 extra by selling the Puts and Calls and have taken no additional risk.

HOW TO PROTECT YOURSELF IN SELLING PUTS OR CALLS

Whether you want to enter the market or not, you can sell puts or Calls and can protect yourself by buying or selling the stock before the Put or Call expires. For example:

Suppose you have sold a Call on U.S Steel at 80 and you are not long or have not bought U. S. Steel. When it advances to 78 or 79 you decide that you do not want to sell it short, as the market looks very strong. In order to protect yourself you buy 100 shares of U.S. Steel at 79. Then, we will assume that at the end of 30 days it closes at 87; the man you sold the Call to demands delivery of the stock and you deliver or sell it to him at 80. You have one point Profit, because you bought it at 79, and you have $112.00 premium money that you received for the Call.

Suppose you sell a Put on U.S. Steel at 72, good 30 days. Then the market turns weak and is declining fast. When it reaches 74, you decide that it acts as if it is going very much lower, and in order to protect yourself you sell 100 shares of U.S. Steel short at 74. Then, we will assume that the stock declines and closes at 69, and that man you sold the Put to at 72, delivers you the stock and 72, which put you out of the market and still gives you a profit of 2 points and the premium money of $112.50.

When you are long of the market or have stocks bought, it is nearly always to your advantage to sell Calls good 30 days until your stock is called, because if you are wrong and the market goes against you, will be taking in the Premium money you receive for the Calls, which will help to cover the loss on the stock.

When you are short of a stock, in most cases it will pay you to sell a Put good for 30 days and take in the money, because if the market declines – as it often does – and fails to reach the Put price, you will still have the money you received for the Put and will still be short of the stock and can sell a Put for next 30 days and take in another $112.50.

I know many traders, when they are long of the market or have stocks bought, who sell Calls every 30 days and sometimes carry the stack for six or twelve months before the man who buys the Calls has an opportunity to call the stock. During all that time they are making more than one point a month profit by selling a Call every 30 days.

BUYING A PUT AND SELLING A CALL AT THE SAME TIME

We will suppose that you buy U.S. Steel at 60 and want to be protected and limit your loss. Then you buy a Put, good 30 days, at 57, which is 3 points under your purchase price; and at the same time you sell a call at 65. This leaves only a small expense or the difference between the Price you sell the Call and the price at which you buy the Put. Should the unexpected happen and some unfavorable news cause U.S. Steel to decline and close at 50 at the end of 30 days, you will be out at 57 because you can deliver on your Put at 57. This is what we call selling a Put or a Call on one side of the market to make the money to pay for protection on the other side.

ARRANGING TO SELL PUTS AND CALLS

You can arrange to sell Puts and Calls by getting in touch with your broker. Any brokerage firm that is a member of the New York Stock Exchange can endorse Puts and Calls. Many firms, however, do not handle this business, but your broker can recommend a firm that will be glad to endorse the Puts and Calls you wish to write. If your broker cannot help you out in this matter, you can get in touch with any member of the Put and Call Dealers Association.

In order to sell a Put or a Call, it is generally necessary that you deposit at least 30% of the value of the stock, or in case of a Call, you can deposit the stock itself, so that the broker will always be protected in case the stock is called for or is put to you.

Puts and Galls are sold not only for 30 days but also for 60 days, 90 days and in some cases for longer periods of time, particularly in dull and inactive markets Also, instead of selling at a regular rate, such as, $125.00 or $112.50, often they are sold for $250, $300, $400, or $500 AT THE MARKET; in other words, instead of getting points up or down, you receive an additional sum of cash which is equivalent to the points.

Your broker or a member of the Put and Call Dealers Association can furnish you with prices and quotations and the details for handling such transactions.

If you will read "How to Make Profits Trading in Puts and Calls" and supplement the information given by the use of charts on a few active stocks, you should be able to protect yourself and also operate a profit in both buying and selling Puts and Calls.

CPSIA information can be obtained
at www.ICGtesting.com
Printed in the USA
LVHW100957010223
738401LV00003B/108